HOW TO FIND A LOVER FRIEND OR COMPANION

A BOOK OF ENCOURAGEMENT

by
Judy Ford
and
William Ashoka Ross

To the truly courageous souls
who remain true to themselves,
and to those who risk embarrassment
by coming to my classes because
their hearts are full of longing,
and to little A. and big B.
and my daughter Amanda,
I dedicate this book.

Copyright © 1988
by Judy Ford and William Ashoka Ross
All rights reserved / Printed in U.S.A.

Playful Wisdom Press
Judy Ford & Company
PO Box 834
Kirkland, WA 98034
For information, call 206/ 823-4421

ISBN 0-9619246-2-4 $4.95

Lov·er, luv'er, *n.* One who loves; a friend or well-wisher. One who has a strong predilection or liking for someone or something. Someone who cares about you.

Most people want to be in a relationship — even the people who want out of the one they're in are hoping for one that will work out better. So wanting a relationship (a lover, a friend, a companion) is normal and natural. Don't apologize for it. And do not pretend you don't care. Instead, congratulate yourself!

For what? For *caring*.

That's right, congratulations! You have taken a step — you're thinking about doing something new. That something new is wanting to reach out to someone. So give yourself a pat on the back — *now!*

You need to congratulate *YOURSELF!*

Some people might think "Shouldn't I congratulate myself *after* I've found a lover?" and I say *no*, dear friend, congratulate yourself *now* for wanting someone new in your life, for admitting it, and for starting to do something about it. After all, don't you think that's the first step? I do.

Millions of people are lonely and want to have lovers in their lives. But you know what? *They won't admit it!* Well, maybe to themselves they admit it (in a quiet and lonely moment) but they don't *do* anything about it. So now hear this:

> **The <u>first</u> step**
>
> **of finding a lover**
>
> *is to admit*
>
> you **want** one.

Otherwise, how will anything ever happen?

4

There is nothing *wrong* with wanting more love in your life. Do you know **anyone** who has enough love in their life? *No one has enough love* — and wanting love is natural and normal. It is *natural* to want a lover, someone who cares about you, in your life. So please don't be ashamed for wanting to have a lover, friend, or companion — and don't try to hide the fact. It's *wonderful* that you want to meet someone to share your life with.

So congratulations to you for admitting it!

When I read a book I always want to know about the author. So let me first of all tell you something personal about myself and what makes me think I know something about this subject. In other words, why am I writing this book? And, *Who Do I Think I Am* to claim I know something about all of this?

WHY AM I WRITING THIS BOOK?
and
Who Do I Think I Am To Claim I Know Something About All Of This?

I want, first of all, to tell you a little story about myself. I collect hearts, and sometimes I wear a few hearts pinned on my jackets and dresses. And one time I had a date and this man said, "You're not going to wear those in public, are you?" And I looked at him and said, "Yes, why not?" And he said, "Well you look *needy* — you look as though you need love!"

Well, of course, the criticism just weighed me down, and I thought all day long, "Oh, he's right! I *am* needy — something's wrong with me." And I thought about this for a good day, and I was feeling bad about myself 'cause it was true, I knew I needed love. I *was* looking for love.

And suddenly that little light bulb went off in my head, and I thought, *"Hey, wait a minute!* What's *wrong* with needing love?" You know, I don't know anybody who has all the love they need. *Do you?* Do you know anybody who has all the love they need? I don't. So I thought, 'Well it's true, I *am* needy, I don't have all the love I need, I need more, I want more — *and what's wrong with admitting it?'*

If you want a new car you admit it, don't you? So what's wrong with admitting you need love? So I'm here to tell you, all of you listening to this, ***that I don't have enough love in my life.* I need more, and I'm open to more love, and I'm not ashamed to admit it.** Yes I do need love — *and when I get enough, I'll tell you!*

So start admitting to yourself and to others that you need love, that you don't have enough love. Because you know what? *They* don't have enough love either. And some people that you come across, they'll pretend that they've got enough — they'll pretend that they don't need **you** and *your* love. But if you remember these words, you'll know that's not so. I haven't met very many people who could honestly say they have enough love in their lives —have you? And I think love is the most precious thing, the most precious commodity, that there is.

My name is Judy Ford and believe me, I never set out to become an expert on relationships. I grew up in a little town in Idaho, and when my high school yearbook came out, what I found printed after my name was *"Never a dull moment."* And that has become my motto. Now, I don't necessarily need a lot of external excitement. I don't need whoop-dee-doo.

But if I have anything to say about it, and I usually do, I will not agree to remain in a boring situation for even ten minutes. I think there is such beauty on this marvelous earth of ours, why should we allow ourselves ever to be bored? That to me is the greatest sin of them all: allowing yourself to be bored. Please don't do it. I truly hope you will respect yourself enough to heed my words. For your sake.

Back to me now. Originally I just wanted to get married and live happily-ever-after with one man. Well, I did that — I met the man of my dreams when I was very young and we were happily married until one fine day he suddenly died of a heart attack.

We were both only 29.

Out of grief and fear, I married my second husband long before I was ready. *Have you ever done something like that? Gotten into a relationship because you were afraid or lonely?* Well, two years later we divorced, and there I was again, single — except now I had a child. Grateful though I was to be the mother of a lovely daughter, one thing I now knew was that I wasn't going to marry again in such a hurry.

I went into therapy. I also enrolled in courses on death and dying with people like Elizabeth Kübler-Ross, read books, studied religion, and dutifully went without sex because my therapist told me to. I even stopped flirting — which, believe me, is not easy for me. I went jogging instead and eventually ran some races. I was very healthy — and very bored.

So I started exploring the world of men.

By this time I was in my early thirties and I'd been single, married, widowed, and divorced. In that order. I'd had every kind of marital status there is.

The question I set for myself was: how could I bring satisfying relationships — satisfying lovers — into my life?

The statistics were against me. They and some of my friends were saying that once you hit 35, it's too late — there aren't enough men available, and so on. But warnings like that just make me more determined!

I decided, first of all, that instead of looking for another person who fit my image and dreams, I would *open to all the wonderful, interesting people in the world — both men and women.* I would create a space inside to connect with people — all kinds of people.

9

Now let me tell you, the friends I made came in all sizes, shapes, ages, philosophies, occupations, financial levels, etc. I threw out my expectations *and I put my focus on exploring and discovering.* I learned by trial and error.

In this book, I am sharing with you some of my personal struggles and those of my clients to bring satisfying relationships into our lives.

I also want you to know I have had periods of desperately wishing I could find someone. I've been in pain and withdrawn. I've been scared and lonely. And through it all I've learned the importance of trusting, going out on a limb, taking a chance, and trying something new. I've often pushed myself when I would have been far more comfortable at home.

I can't give you any guarantees that the things this book will bring you a special someone. Because finding a lover, friend or companion is not an engineering project. You see, there is something *magical* about finding a lover. It's an unknown something that happens — a surprise, a special moment — a little miracle. So...

**I know it's scary
and sometimes
trying something new is
OVERWHELMING
but
YOU CAN DO IT**
so . . .
take a deep breathe and plunge ahead!

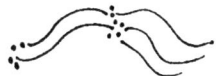

The first thing I want you to do is consider this question, and you must do it alone, when you have 15 minutes of quiet time all by your self. Ask yourself this question and listen quietly for the answer.

> Do you think it's possible
> for you to bring
> a lover,
> friend
> or companion
> into your life?

Now listen quietly for the answer. Don't just accept the first answer that pops into your head. Consider this question carefully. If you answered *Yes!* to the depth of your soul, then you are ready to move on.

If you answered **No**, then I want you to carefully consider this. If you *don't* believe it's possible, then it is *not* possible, and no amount of outside action will change your reality. *Everything is possible.* Regardless of what the statistics say, it is possible for you to create whatever your heart desires, and you must know this to make it happen for yourself. If you know this is true, then the work becomes fun. This is called **Possibility Thinking**.

And possibility thinking is packed with power and energy.

How To Find A Lover, both the book and the activity, is divided into two themes or aspects. The *inner* work and the *outer* work. The outer work consists of "Where-do-you-go?" and "What-do-you-say?" The inner work is what you do on the inside to *really* make things happen. And friends, I am convinced that the inner work is often *especially* important. The inner work is the real key if you want to connect deeply with a special someone.

And what is the inner work?

✓ I think the most important part of the inner work is developing a *trust in the process of life.* Some call it faith. When we lose faith or trust, what happens is that we become frantic. Frantic, of course, feels awful and produces more frantic, as well as panic and fear. It becomes a very vicious circle. When we focus our attention too closely on "finding someone," the focus is too much outside ourselves. What happens is that we then lose contact with ourselves, with what we are thinking and feeling, with our own *power*. This creates great disharmony within us and that, of course, feels awful and results in more panic and desperateness.

I think when we feel desperate, in a state of panic, or in a state of hopelessness, that's when we have our worst moments. I think the most important thing all we humans have to learn to deal with is our desperateness and panic and lack of faith.

In a way, the inner work becomes the focus and the outer work becomes almost the by-product. So put the focus on your faith and trust! Then, when your confidence is reasonably strong, *take action!* As the telephone company says, "Reach out and touch someone!" And remember, as you make yourself more confident, you will certainly become more radiant. Then you'll feel better and also feel better *about yourself,* and others will naturally notice that. Then how long do you think it can really be before some wonderful things begin to happen for you?

When you are afraid,
admit it,
and when you are full of doubts,
admit that, too,
at least to yourself.
When you are in despair,
don't just run away —
admit it to yourself,
and then
find a little faith and
a little trust that
Life Will Work Out
For You —
work out for you just right,
and I'll bet you anything
that it *will!*

Now, first of all:

You've Admitted To Yourself
You Want To Bring A New
SOMEONE
Into Your Life

Right? Well, that is a great beginning! And now, before you take outside action, you must do a little internal work first. This is very important because frequently old attitudes and beliefs sabotage our efforts so that we can't get what we want. Lets check it out.

PERSONAL INVENTORY
(DO YOU HAVE ANY OF THESE IDEAS?)

1. THE "RIGHT PERSON" SYNDROME. This is the idea that there is a "right-person" for you. You may even have a mental picture of them. This is dangerous because you may reject those who *don't* measure up to your mental image.

2. THE "HAPPY-EVER AFTER" THEORY. Lots of fairytales end like this, but not real life. Too many people believe that once you've found each other the work is done and now happiness is assured. This is a dangerous theory. Look at the divorce statistics! You have to *work* at a relationship to make it succeed.

3. THE "YOU ARE ALL I NEED" HYPOTHESIS. Many people are convinced that once they find the other person, they won't need anyone else in their lives. Frequently they demand that their partner be totally available only to them. They get rid of their own former friends and stop doing the things they used to enjoy doing on their own. This can put a lot of stress and strain on the relationship and often leads to boredom and restlessness. So watch out for this tendency.

4. THE "SOMETHING WRONG WITH ME" BLUES. You have a feeling that something is wrong with you. Like you're too fat or too bald. You have a crooked nose and the house you live in is messy and the furniture is old. Your stomach isn't flat and your feet aren't the same size. You don't make much money and you've never been to Europe. You can't make interesting conversation and even if you could think of something clever, no one would listen. *Beware!* This kind of thinking can really defeat you before you begin. You don't have to have all those things fixed first. Trust me here!

5. THE "BUT ALL THE GOOD ONES ARE MARRIED" DOLDRUMS. You are convinced that all the good ones are taken, or else you would prefer someone younger or thinner. You have read the statistics and you know it is too late for you. You spend most nights in front of the VCR complaining to friends about the creeps out there, but secretly you hope you will find someone.

6. THE "BUT I DON'T WANT TO GET HURT AGAIN" MORASS. You have been hurt and rejected — maybe once, maybe ten times — and you remember the hurt and embarrassment. Somehow it's still fresh and you want to avoid that again. Just remember: so has everyone else and they don't want to be rejected either, but *someone* has to make the move or you will never connect. Take a chance that you'll survive!

7. THE "I'LL BE HAPPY WHEN" DELUSION. Some people have the idea that they'll be happywhen they find the right person. They tend to postpone their happiness until then and don't do anything *now*. You can do some things for yourself *now* which will definitely make you happier. If you make yourself happier, you will become even more attractive! So don't *wait* for someone else to make you happy.

8. THE "ASHAMED TO BE SINGLE" FIXATION. Some people feel it is such a failure to be single that they never go any place as a single person. They always need a friend or acquaintance to accompany them. Oh, sometimes they may go to a matinee by themselves, but never any place where someone might notice that they're alone. This is subtle but dangerous if you're single and want to meet someone else who is single. There is nothing to be ashamed of here. Your are an *independent* person; be proud of that!

OKAY!
YOU HAVE DONE YOUR PERSONAL INVENTORY
YOU HAVE FOUND SOME OF THE IDEAS
THAT COULD CREATE A FEW

ROADBLOCKS

BE SURE TO WORK THESE OUT!

DEPENDING ON HOW ENTRENCHED THESE
IDEAS ARE,
**YOU MAY NEED TO REFLECT DEEPLY
OR SEE A COUNSELOR
<u>TO BREAK OUT OF THESE
OUTMODED WAYS OF THINKING</u>**

THAT'S REALLY IMPORTANT
IF YOU WANT TO GO ON
TO SOMETHING NEW

You've done a lot of work so far. You've given this a lot of thought. **Keep going!**

Now decide what you want, but remember *nothing is written in stone* — so you can change your mind at any time! What we're doing right now is just to help you get clear about what is important to you. Here is the fundamental question:

WHAT DO YOU WANT?

1. A SEX PARTNER — Someone you call for sex whenever you're "in the mood." There is an understanding between you that this is *not* the relationship of your dreams — but the sexual energy is right and it's working for you *now*. So please don't dismiss the value of this type of relationship too soon. A client of mine, recovering from a painful divorce in which her self-esteem was shattered, told me she needed a sex partner again not only to find out if she was attractive to men, but also to find out *"if her equipment still worked."* **Outcome**: this kind of arrangement probably won't last, but you'll have had some thrilling times and chances are you'll feel like new.

2. A ROMANTIC ENCOUNTER — The romance is great! You act like a teen infatuated for the first time. There is lots of energy between you and the excitement is high. You have meaningful conversations and every embrace is indescribable. *Outcome:* could go either way, depending on whether the two of you also agree in other areas.

3. A FRIENDSHIP LOVER — You like each other and you feel appreciated and cared for by the other person. They see the best in you. You see the good in them. You also have fun together. *Outcome:* Lots of potential for mutual satisfaction, but it does take work if you want to create some magic.

In the classes that I teach on this subject, people always ask me why I didn't include a category for 'spouse'. Well, I'll leave the marital status up to you. What I really want you to consider is the *type* of relationships you want in your life. So if you want to, you can marry any of the above categories — that's entirely up to you.

Here's a surprising fact I want you to consider:

When you don't know what you want, you *always* get what you *don't* want.

If you think about it, you'll see that that's true. Soooo . . . it's *extremely* important that you make up your mind and answer the following question:

WHAT IS YOUR HEART'S DESIRE?

Now Tell The Truth!

Remember, it is *highly* important to have clear ideas about what qualities are important to you!

I'm going to tell you a true story about a woman client of mine. She came to me for therapy when she was unhappily married, and we worked together for about a year. Initially, she didn't know why she was unhappy. After all, her husband was good looking and successful. He cared very much for the children, and he took an active role in parenting. They had a lovely house in the suburbs, they had an active social life — but despite all this she was deeply unhappy.

Well, what she discovered was that she *couldn't talk to her husband!* He wasn't interested in hearing her point of view — or even her thoughts and feelings. He had a definite idea of how he wanted his life to be; he had created that very successfully. He talked to her at length about his projects and never seemed to care (or even notice) that she wasn't doing much talking herself. After a while they divorced.

About a year after her divorce, she came back to therapy. This time she was concerned that she wasn't having satisfying relationships. She was dating a lot and many men were interested in her, but she had the same sick feeling with them that she had with her husband. She couldn't put her finger on what was wrong but something was missing. She *wanted* a satisfying relationship but she didn't seem to be able to find one.

I asked her,

"What qualities do you want in a partner?"

Well, much to my surprise she had them listed and was actually carrying them in her purse! She pulled the list out and read it to me. She had listed 'good looking,' 'ambitious,' 'financially successful,' 'physically active.' And do you know, *all the men she was dating fit that description and she still wasn't satisfied!* So I asked her, "What about **understanding?** Don't you want your man to be understanding, patient, caring, loving, open, warm?" I pointed out to her that none of the qualities she had listed were important for having a nurturing, close, personal relationship.

Well she was shocked! She saw that she was getting exactly what was on her list, but that it wasn't nurturing. Later she reordered her priorities and revised her list. So my advice to you, too, is *think about it!* **Re-think your priorities!** What qualities do *you* want? And don't leave out the very qualities that make a relationship really worth while.

A friend of mine told me that when she was in her twenties, what she wanted was a good looking football player who made a lot of money and had a great body. But now that she was in her thirties and had some life experience under her belt, she realized that what she really wanted was *"someone who likes me"* —someone who cared about her and was interested in her.

It isn't uncommon for people to become suspicious if someone likes them. They wonder if there isn't something 'wrong' with such a person. I have heard many people say, "Well if she or he likes me, they're not my type." Some people seem to need to find someone who *will* reject them. Please don't fall into this trap.

Get really clear about what you want — that's the *best* way you will increase your chances!

Now here is your homework assignment. I want you to list some qualities that are important to you — qualities that you want in a lover. And the first quality on that list must be:

SOMEONE WHO LIKES ME!

So now go ahead and list some of the other qualities. This way you'll be constructing a profile of the kind of person you want:

_____

_____

_____

_____

_____

Now ask yourself what this person's life-style might be like. Is he a skier? Does he like the ocean? Does he or she have children? All of that information will come in handy when we try to figure out where you're going to meet this person.

WELL, THAT'S GOOD!
YOU'VE THOUGHT THINGS OVER,
AND YOU NOW HAVE SOME IDEA
OF WHAT YOU WANT

Now it's time for action! You can't sit there, you have to *do* something. This is where most people really get scared. But keep going: you can make a lot of very nice things happen. You can make new friends and have some wonderful new experiences. Just take a chance!

TAKING ACTION

Now Is The Time For Action

&
YOU CAN DO IT ...

YOU <u>CAN</u> DO IT!

Now I'm going to tell you some interesting stories about how some people I know met. Then I'll suggest some places to go and some things to try. Then it will be your turn to come up with what you are going to do.

INTERESTING TRUE STORIES

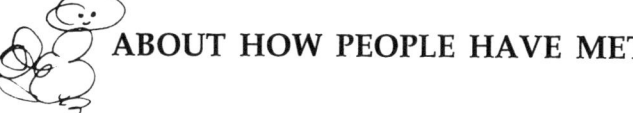 ## ABOUT HOW PEOPLE HAVE MET

I know a business woman who met a man at a conference. They were discussing a subject of interest to both of them. Just before they went their separate ways, the woman asked: "Would you like me to let you know the outcome of this project?" "Yes," he replied, "I certainly would." They exchanged business cards. Several weeks later she called him to report. They met for lunch and their romance began.

(Speaking of business cards, I think it is a good idea to have some made for yourself. Even if the work you do does not require them. I had some made for a single friend of mine with her home phone number. This way she can give them to anyone she wants. Such cards could also include a saying, a motto, or a design. Just use your imagination!)

I know a woman who worked at a large hospital. She kept running into a man from another department. She found him very attractive but she didn't know his name. Because she knew people at hospitals gossip a lot, she didn't want to ask anyone. So she had a friend of hers call his department. The friend said that the young man (whom she described) had cared for her that day and had been so polite and helpful that she wanted to write a letter to the hospital to thank him. Could she please have his name? She was given his name.

Now, finally, this woman at least knew the attractive man's name! The next time she saw him, she was able to call him by name. Soon they had their first date. They developed a good friendship and now do lots of things together.

I know a man and woman, both single parents, who met at a fast food restaurant on a Saturday afternoon. They told me that this is a great place to meet other single parents — just look for the adult alone with a couple of kids and start a conversation. They are probably eager for some adult conversation!

I know a married couple who met on a bus. They both rode the same bus to work every day. One day they connected...

Grocery stores are good, especially at six o'clock at night — that's when all the single people seem to do their shopping. Speaking of grocery stores, I know a woman who met her husband because he saw her name on her checkbook when she paid for her groceries. He called her up an hour later and said, "Hey, instead of cooking all that food I just saw you buy" (and he named it item by item) "wouldn't you rather go out to dinner?"

If you're brave, you can do what a friend of mine did. She met her husband while riding an elevator. She had seen him several times in this particular building and noticed that he wasn't wearing a wedding ring! So believe it or not, she went back every day for about two weeks until they met in the elevator. She spoke with him and gave him her business card (see, those business cards come in handy) and the rest is matrimonial history.

One day a friend of mine was listening to a disk jockey on the radio. She heard him say he was single. Well, she called him! She was feeling very embarrassed, but she went to the radio station to meet him. And they got married!

The well known author Ayn Rand met her husband when she was an unknown extra in one of Cecil B. DeMille's movies. It was love at first sight. She met him in a very unromantic way — they were both standing in line one day to cash their paychecks. She thought about him for months, until one day, "just by chance," she wandered into a public library — and there he was. Their marriage lasted for over thirty years.

The whole point of these little stories is that you can meet people *anyplace*. *All* places are magical! Yes, some places *are* more romantic than others, but you can meet lovers at work, where you live, and where you normally play. And there is no 'off season.' You just have to keep your eyes open and be willing to take a chance — and (this is *very* important) know that you can back out at any moment!

HOMEWORK ASSIGNMENT

I want you to start experimenting and see how many people *you* can make contact with this week. *Don't change your normal routine* — instead, see for yourself how many people you can make contact with that previously you've dismissed as uninteresting.

You can meet people *anyplace*. Single people are everywhere. I know one couple who met at a PTA meeting! Opportunities abound, so keep your eyes open and stay alert.

Now here are some more ideas of where to meet people:

• **Flying Kites in the Park.** Ask someone who looks interesting to help you unravel the string or attach the tail.

• **Singles Bars.** Singles bars are the places where single people hang out hoping to meet other singles — while pretending they don't want to meet *anyone.* Many act disinterested and cool and then feel disappointed that they were unable to connect. If you go to a singles bar, for heaven's sakes *talk* to people, and don't pretend that it doesn't matter. You are there because you want to meet someone and there is nothing wrong with that. (Be aware that some marrieds disguise themselves as single. Also that this atmosphere may feel pushy and competitive.)

• **Classes.** If you are a man, take a sewing class. If you're a woman, take a course in building a log home. Get the idea? Now for heaven's sakes, when you take a class never, *never* walk into the classroom and grab the first seat you can see, and never be the first person to take a seat. When you walk in, *check out the other people in the class!* Look them over and find someone interesting and sit by them. Then be sure and start a conversation. Even if the class meets again, be sure to get their phone number and give them yours.

- **Singles Clubs and Organizations.** Now don't knock this before you try a few. It is true that some have more women than men, so men, you can have a great time! I met a very nice man at a singles' organization and although we went our separate ways, the experience enriched my life.

- **Restaurants.** Be daring and eat some meals out alone. I know singles who have coffee at the same restaurant every morning. The idea is that after a while of being in the same place at the same time each day, they know they will get to know other people.

- **Personal Ads.** This can be great fun! Writing a personal ad is a marvelous growth experience. It is a highly useful exercise to put down on paper what it is that *you* have to offer that is appealing. That is a wonderful discipline. I do suggest, however, that you don't do any out and out lying. And remember, if what you write doesn't sound good, you can always start over again until you get **"you"** right.

- **At Work.** Lots of couples have met here. Just weigh the consequences of getting involved with someone in this environment. If the risk isn't too high — *go for it!*

- **In Your Neighborhood.** As Mr. Rogers sings "Who are the people in your neighborhood, your neighborhood, your neighborhood? Who are the people in your neighborhood, the people that you meet each day?" Make sure you know — there could be some really neat ones that you've been overlooking.

- **Friends.** If you haven't already, be sure to let your friends know you are open to having them connect you with someone.

- **Start Your Own Club.** This is my favorite idea! I once, with a friend, started something called **The Grey Beard Club**. The club was open to *"anyone who has ever had a gray beard, loved someone with a gray beard, or who would like to."* I also formed a club called the **Run For Brunch Bunch.** We'd meet on Sundays, run about three miles, and then go to brunch! Many people in my classes are now forming their own clubs and I do the advertising for them. Everything from sailing, gourmet dining, TV watching, to investing. My advice is: form the kind of club that will attract people you want to meet. This way *you* can make the rules and screen the members.

Additional Places To Go:

- **Join a Computer Club.** Computers are everywhere and so are computer clubs — and they are jammed full of people, especially men. Join *any* kind of club, from astronomy to zebra-watching — if you're interested in it, there's probably a club for it.

- **Join a Cooking Class.** That's usually a good way of meeting women! Learn some unusual ethnic cooking — Chinese food has great appeal, and so does Indian in some circles. And it's an irresistible invitation to be able to say, "I'm cooking some Indonesian food, would you like to come?"

- **University Classes.** University classes are a good spot. Night classes at a community college etc. People of all ages go to school these days. To learn and to meet.

- **Become Active in a Cause.** I know numerous couples who have met working on a campaign or for some movement like "Save the Whales." And there's no shortage of good causes. It makes *sense* to try to do something about the dumping of toxic wastes, and you can meet some very wonderful people that way.

- **In the Library.** Libraries are full of both men and women. Some are doing research for a book, some reading newspapers from other cities, some looking through magazines they don't subscribe to. Be sure to check out the various libraries in your city to find out which one draws what crowd. Lots of libraries have free courses. Find one and attend.

- **Watching TV.** Yes, believe it or not, I once met a man while I was alone in my house watching TV! I saw a man on TV whom I found delightful and inspiring. Without knowing anything about him I wrote him a letter. Well, he called me long distance! It turned out he was single, which I didn't know when I wrote. We struck up a friendship on the phone and he later flew to Seattle to take me out to dinner. The energy wasn't right for a romantic encounter, but we continue to be friends and he still calls me occasionally.

- **Stores.** Book stores are great for meeting people. Provided, of course, that you are willing to start a conversation with a stranger. Lots of people claim grocery stores, liquor stores, supermarkets, sports stores, video stores, even shoe stores, are excellent meeting spots. Here again you have to be willing to *say* something and *look* at the person and *smile*.

- **Become A Volunteer.** All the social service agencies have volunteer boards of directors, so get on the board of directors of some organization or get involved in fund-raising for your favorite charity. I know some people who have met some very wealthy people doing this.

- **Churches.** Some churches have active singles organizations. You'll have to do some research here to find a church where you feel comfortable.

- **Dance Classes.** Join some Dance Classes. *Men:* if you want to meet women, join a Dance Class, women love to dance. And whether it's aerobics, square dancing, rock, jazz or tango, there are usually more women than men, so you can have a field day while getting great exercise.

- **Take Up A Sport.** Keep in mind that team sports are much better for meeting people than sports like tennis where you basically only meet one partner. High energy sports like skiing are great because where there's high energy, there's lots of socializing. So learn to ski, to swim, to play volley ball, bowl, skydive, windsurf, or whatever. Check out whatever classes exist in your area; ask the instructor how many people are in them *and what their sex is.* Even if you have to drive clear across town, getting into a class that is populated by the sex *you* want to meet will be well worth the effort.

- **Roller Skating Rinks.** Check out your Roller Skating Rinks. Call them up and ask if they have an adult only night. Then go!

- **Chamber Of Commerce.** Call the Chamber Of Commerce and get involved in some way. Remember, business can be very exciting — and so can a lot of business people, provided you give them the right sort of encouragement!

- **Video Dating.** There are places where you can go and place a video tape of yourself on file. In return (and a fee of several hundred dollars) you can screen the video tapes of others until you find the kind of person who appeals to you. Here's my advice: don't sign up for more than one year, even if it's a cut-rate bargain — *you might not need to!*

- **Do Some Research.** Now you have to do some research in your area on the best places to go and connect with others. So you're going to research this, *and while you're researching, you might actually meet somebody!* Start asking people where *they* go to meet other people — do it as though you were doing marketing research, which you are! Ask them about organizations they belong to and what the members are like. Then go to the library and ask the librarian to give you the listing of all the clubs and organizations in the area. Find some that are interesting to you and start checking those out. Read your local newspaper to get ideas about what is going on in your community. Attend lectures, go to concerts. If you have a zoo, volunteer at the zoo.

I have given you a lot of interesting ideas but there are a lot more.

Now *you* think of a few new things you want to try. Below, list some new things you're going to try, or something you like doing but haven't done in a while.

Write them here:

1. _____

2. _____

3. _____

4. _____

5. _____

OKAY, THAT'S GREAT!!

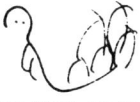

NOW WHICH ONE ARE YOU GOING TO DO *THIS* WEEK — NOT NEXT WEEK????

_____

_____

_____

That's good. Isn't this exciting? You are taking action and bringing new friends into your life. Break out the champagne!

NOW, DON'T CHICKEN OUT!
MAKE A DECISION AND TAKE
ACTION
THIS WEEK

And now we get to something highly important:

THE IMPORTANCE OF TAKING RISKS, SAYING NO, AND GOING OUT ALONE

When looking for a lover, you've got to learn to take a risk — you know, take a chance — and then, when you learn that, you'll also have to learn to say no. Saying no means simply saying, *"No, I don't want to."* Because why would anyone want to take a risk if they weren't able to say no? The two go hand in hand. So does going out alone.

All the things I'm going to tell you about in this section — which I want you to start doing — will lead you closer to the person you're looking for.

TAKING RISKS

Now suppose you were at a party, and you saw an attractive man or woman talking with a group of people. What would you do? Would you:

- **Hope the person would notice you?**

- **Hope that the group of people would thin out so you could join in?**

- **Hope that the conversation would end?**

What *would* you do? Would you just shrug it off and say, 'Well, maybe next time?' Or would you take a chance and risk something? And what would risking mean to you? Would you be willing to go over and join the conversation? Would you be willing to go directly to the person you're attracted to and start talking to them? Or would you ask somebody to introduce you to the attractive person? Would you be willing to find out the person's phone number and call them later?

If you want a lover in your life, you've got to take a risk. Yes, it's true you may get rejected, you may even get laughed at, *but are you **willing** to take a chance, to gamble, to go for it?*

When it comes to love and attraction, there is *always* an element of risk. Playing it safe may bring security; it does *not* bring love. So unless you're happy being alone, you'll always have to be willing to take a risk.

Which brings us to the next question — or rather, questions, plural. There are two questions that are frequently asked in my class on **How To Find A Lover.** Frequently people will raise their hands and say,

"But what if I make a fool of myself?"

The other question is:

"What if I decide I don't want to be with this person?"

Well that is very simple — you can *always* change your mind! You can *always* say no. Why, you can even change your mind when the man has his pants off and is ready to jump into bed with you! *Yes, you can!* Or when a woman is nibbling on your ear and obviously wants you to make love to her. If in that moment you decide you really *don't* want to, it's perfectly OK to change your mind and say so.

You see, taking a risk goes hand in hand with becoming able to say no. *No one* would ever take the risk of approaching a stranger, someone you don't know *anything* about, if they thought this meant they were committed. You really must let yourself realize this, it's so important.

Just because you *talk* to someone or approach them, it doesn't mean you're committed to going out with them — and it certainly doesn't mean you have to go to bed with someone you don't want to go to bed with.

Do you feel obliged to go to bed with somebody just because they've been nice to you? Would *you* go to bed with somebody just because they cooked you a beautiful dinner and entertained you? I wouldn't — not if I didn't really want to. But you have to be willing to say so. If you're not willing to say no, then you'll find yourself in a fine pickle — and you'll <u>never</u> take a chance on something new, *because you'll be afraid you won't be able to get out of it if you don't like it!* So remember the importance of saying no —

Close your eyes...

and imagine these words imprinted in your mind:

THE IMPORTANCE OF SAYING NO

or

IT'S <u>IMPORTANT</u> TO BE WILLING TO SAY NO!

Then repeat five times:

"I can say no to *anybody* !"

And any time you find yourself in a situation you don't want to be in, close your eyes and remember that saying! Remember that saying no is extremely important in finding a lover. When you remember that, then you'll be brave and be able to say no in *any* situation.

LEARN TO GO OUT ALONE!

If you are used to going places on your own then you can ignore this one. But if your *aren't*, then pay attention. After my husband died, one of the first things that I became painfully aware of was how much my free time, my entertainment and social life, revolved around him. Now I was really stuck — I had never even been to a movie by myself! So one Sunday I decided to venture forth and believe me, this was hard, I was so scared. I was sure everyone would be looking at me and thinking, *"How come that poor lady is all alone?"* For me, at that time, this was a big embarrassment.

Anyway I went to the movie on a Sunday afternoon and stood in line with the others. Of course everyone seemed to be in couples. I felt like the only odd ball. Well, I made it into the theater and I wanted to buy some popcorn. But here again I was afraid and insecure. What would the girl behind the counter think of me, buying popcorn for myself? If I just bought *one* bag then she would know for sure that I was alone. So you know what I did, I bought *two* bags of popcorn and *two* drinks. Yes I did! That is how bad off I was. Well, fortunately I've come a long way since. And now, going to the movies by myself is a favorite activity for me — I love going to the movies alone. So take this advice:

DO SOMETHING
YOU HAVE NEVER DONE BEFORE
— AND DO IT ALONE!

Now here is something important for you to know!

Eye-Contact

Yes, that's right: *eye-contact*.

Eye-contact is <u>very</u> important. People have been across crowded rooms and gotten off their chairs to meet one another because of eye-contact. I know because it happened to me once. Try it. And also when you are meeting someone — don't just stare off into space or at the floor. *Look* at the person you're meeting. Look right into their eyes and smile!

Energy/Vibe

You know, it really doesn't matter *what* you say or even so much how you're dressed (clean and comfortable is important, though) compared to the energy vibe between you. *Does being around this person feel **good**? Are you feeling **drawn** to the other person? Is the energy **flowing** between you?* Energy is always much more important than words. So don't concentrate so much on the looks and the words, focus on the energy and how the encounter *feels*. Sometimes people can look great, can be dressed in the latest style and say lots of clever things — but they feel awful to be around. That's because their energy tells you something is wrong. Pay attention to that; it's very important. And take a look at your own vibe. Do you put out a vibe that says "stay away?" Are you closed? Is your vibe one that draws people to you or does it push them away?

Touch

You can let a person know that you're interested in them as well as checking how they feel by a light, friendly, warm touch. Dancing is a socially accepted way of touching someone, but I'm also taking about that light touch on someone's shoulder or a gentle hand squeeze, or even lightly touching the knee.

A <u>lot</u> can be said without words!
Learn the language of

Eye-Contact
Energy
& Touch

and you can save yourself a lot of needless worry over **"Did I say the right thing?"**

Oh yes! One more thing. *Don't forget to flirt!* Regardless of what anyone may tell you or has ever told you, flirting is the innocent expression of playful aliveness and not at all 'sinful' (as I and so many others were taught when we were growing up). Flirting is enjoyable and it adds lots of excitement and zest to any encounter. Please don't ever let anyone put you down for flirting!

THE ART OF FLIRTING

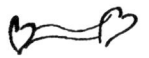

When was the last time you flirted? Was it today, yesterday, last week, this month, this year, or so long ago that you can't remember? Well, if your answer is any longer than a few days ago, you're getting rusty!

To find a lover, you have to flirt with someone *every* week. And everybody goes about it differently. Some people are too embarrassed to admit they like it. Others are brazen and bold about it and very obvious. Some people use the sly, seductive approach. Flirting is very important in catching a lover. *It's part of nature to flirt* — peacocks strut, and birds flutter — and besides being natural, *it's fun*. So I want you to start flirting. Some of you may say you don't know how, but I don't believe it, I think it's just that you forgot due to some embarrassment.

The dictionary says flirting is **"to behave amorously without serious intent."** I guess that's why flirting got its bad name. Because flirting isn't serious at all — flirting is fun! It's the people who take it *seriously* who give flirting a bad name. Seriousness is the opposite of playfulness. And amorous? When you see that *'amorous'* is simply another word for *'loving,'* why shouldn't we be amorous? Doesn't religion teach us to be loving?

Flirting is simply letting another person know that you're interested in being playful. It's a fun way to let someone know you're interested in them. It's not necessarily about romance or sex. It's a way to get a friendship started — it's sort of the ground-breaking, a little bridge from you to them. Now some people don't like flirting, and people who flirt sometimes have a bad reputation, and the reason may be that the person who flirts doesn't know when to stop. *Don't flirt with someone who doesn't flirt back* — it's a waste of time. If they don't flirt back, stop. Remember that flirting is the way two people let each other know they're interested in being playful. If someone doesn't flirt back, they're probably not in the mood for fun. Remember, even listening intently to what another person is saying can be a way of flirting

Have you ever seen a baby play peek-a-boo? First they get your attention. They get you to look at them. Then... they cover their face with their hands! Then they peek out to see if you're still looking. They giggle and smile and cover their face again with their little hands. And if you'll keep looking at them and cover your face with *your* hands and peek out at them, the game can continue for quite a while. If you ignore the baby, they'll just find someone else who's more willing to play peek-a-boo.

Flirting is sort of like this. It's like a little game of peek-a-boo. If you think of flirting and start to get scared, think of yourself as a baby and the other person as a baby and realize that all you're doing is playing peek-a-boo! Flirting is just peek-a-boo for adults.

Some people have stopped flirting for fear of being called a tease. Or they are afraid that if they flirt with someone, they will have to continue and "go all the way." Well, that just is not so. You can flirt and have a good time with someone and *you can stop at any time.* Flirting is fun and you can stop whenever you want.

When was the last time you flirted? When do you want the next time to be?

THE BIGGEST OBSTACLE TO FINDING A LOVER

I was doing one of my **How To Find A Lover** classes when a man asked, "What do I have to offer?"

Now that was a very courageous question! You can think of it as due to timidity, shyness, or maybe you can call it an inferiority complex, but that's how he felt. And since then I've discovered that *a lot of people* feel this way. Many, many people have told me they feel they don't really have anything to offer. Now, isn't that a shocking discovery? Individuals who feel they don't have anything to offer to another human being! — and let me tell you, some of them were very nice, prosperous, nice looking, talented, well-dressed people.

And since that evening, I've realized that it's this outlook, this way of seeing yourself, that keeps people alone and lonely. *Nothing else.* And do you know, it's such an unnecessary way of looking at things. It's all based on a few simple mistaken ideas. And if you give me just a few minutes, I'm going to explain that to you.

First of all, I want you to look around at the people you know. Look at who's married to whom. And what's the first thing you'll think when you do that? You'll think:

"I wonder what he ever sees in her??"

Won't you? Because it will immediately be clear to you that the people who are in relationships *have all the defects (and more) that you think of yourself as having!*

Look around! You'll see couples where the wife is too fat or doesn't have a brain in her head, where the husband is a flop at making a living, drinks, and maybe is bad–tempered in the bargain. Or you'll see couples where the wife is always whining or crying, or where the man is always "putting his foot down," whatever that means. This one's bald, that one's paunchy, the other has a big nose, somebody else has bad breath or a speech defect — and so on.

Now, do you think those people have a great deal to offer?

Well, if *those* people have something to offer (and they obviously do, or no one would be with them) don't you think *you* have something to offer??

And don't forget there are also people who are severely handicapped. Some of them are in a wheelchair. *But does that stop some of these people from having a relationship?* No, it doesn't! I know of a paraplegic who has no problem at all finding lovers — he always has a beautiful woman with him. So the bottom line is that lame people find lovers, blind people find lovers, deaf people find lovers, impotent people find lovers, and you think *you* don't have anything to offer??

There's only one kind of person who doesn't have anything to offer...

...and that's a person who doesn't love. But that's not true of you, otherwise you would not be reading this book. **Would an unloving person want to learn how to find a lover?** *Would an unloving person take courses and classes and go to therapy and counseling to find out how to improve their relationships?* I don't think so. Not the ones I've seen.

So you see, you *are* a loving person. And you *have* something to offer! So please give up whatever guilt you may still be hanging on to. *Guilt is for the birds!*

Now, here's an exercise I want you to do. It's a sentence completion exercise, and an extremely important and rewarding one. It may look easy, but believe me, if you really do it you'll find it's anything but easy. Here it is:

As a woman/man, what I have to offer is...

_____

_____

_____

_____

Remember, *you can't lie to yourself!* You can't convince yourself you're desirable if deep down you feel you don't have much to offer. You can try to present yourself however you want to when it comes to others, but you can't deceive *yourself* — not for long, anyway. I've tried to kid myself, and I know others who have too, but it never seems to work, and it *can't*. We **know** how we feel about ourselves and we can't get away from it. If you feel like Cinderella before she met the Prince, then you need to deal with that. Just know that Superman (and woman) aren't the only ones who have something to offer — Clark Kent and whoever his female counterpart is do too!

We all have something to offer, we just have to find it. So this exercise will bring you more in touch with what you genuinely feel you have to offer. And **_knowing_** that you really do have something to offer instantly makes you more confident, happier — and more loving!

Yes, we can all learn to become more loving — but we don't have to be loving to *everybody* all the time. Love is something that grows in you, not something you're born with. You don't have to be perfect right from the start.

Now let me tell you of one thing that you *do* have to offer — something that *everyone* has to offer. It may seem insignificant to you but let me tell you, it's very important. What is it? It's this:

The greatest thing you have to offer — and I want you to imagine me writing this on a blackboard — is:

THE WILLINGNESS TO BE REAL

That's the greatest gift one human being can give to another! Did you know that? You don't have to offer diamonds or gems, you don't have to be the greatest gourmet cook, you don't have to be a superman or superwoman in the bedroom.

The greatest, the most appreciated gift one person can make to another is the willingness to be real. *Yes, the willingness to be real!* **People are starved for that, even when they don't know it! Because only being real is really nourishing — not phoniness.**

Phoniness doesn't work. It's old hat. Everyone is tired of it and it does not succeed.

Now, you may not believe that statement. Maybe you've thought that in this world you have to be a phony to succeed. Well, being a phony may pay off in some respects but believe me, *phoniness does not pay off in relationships*. Being phony may attract people — I don't say it doesn't — but it won't help you *sustain* a satisfying relationship. If seduction is what you're after, phoniness works. But seduction is a short-term proposition. If you're into seduction, you'll need to seduce again and again — it goes with the territory. But believe me, it's hard work and I don't think it pays off. If you want a satisfying relationship, nothing beats being real.

Being real nourishes and being unreal doesn't.

So please think about that and realize the precious gift you have to offer your lover, this willingness to be real. You may not achieve it 100% — that doesn't matter. You don't have to be 100% honest. The willingness to be real instantly deepens the bond between you and another person — even if some of the words you speak aren't completely accurate.

There's a passage in Margery Williams' *The Velveteen Rabbit*, which is one of my favorite books. It's when the Velveteen Rabbit asks the Skin Horse what "real" means.

"Real isn't how you are made," said the Skin Horse. "it's a thing that happens to you. When a child loves you for a long, long time, not just to play with but REALLY loves you, then you become real."

"Does it hurt?" asked the Rabbit.

"Sometimes," said the Skin Horse, for he was always very truthful. "But when you are real you don't mind being hurt."

And that's my experience too.

So never, *never* make the mistake of thinking you don't have anything to offer. ***Everyone has something to offer!*** The only difference between them and you is that now you know it. Now you can do something about it.

Practice the art of becoming real! And realize that there are many, *many* lovers out there in the world who are hungry, starved, for what *you* can provide.

OPENING LINES

A lot of people have asked me, *"When I see somebody I like — what do I say?"* Particularly if it's in a situation where you don't have much time — *how* do you get the conversation going ? How do you let the person know you want to talk to them?

Talking to strangers comes hard for a lot of us, but when you want to find a lover, it's a skill that you'll want to practice because it requires practice. So first of all, *you'll have to be bold!* If you're going to wait until you feel comfortable, you'll probably miss your chance. Even though you feel scared and are shaking in your boots, you've got to do it anyway.

Now for example, if I'm standing in a line at the movie theater next to someone who I think is attractive, I try to start the conversation with something relevant. It can be something obvious, as simple as:

"This sure is a long line!"

Then you might say, "I can hardly wait to get some popcorn, are you going to get some popcorn?" Or: "What made you choose this movie?" Or: "Where do you like to sit inside the movie — do you have a favorite place you like to sit?" "Do you like to come to the movies alone?" And then you might laugh and say, *"I hope you don't mind talkative strangers."* And if they're the kind of persons who are good for you, they won't mind.

All conversation starters need to be in a light-hearted spirit, a spirit of jest and fun. Because the spirit with which you say these things will be what will make the difference — not your cleverness.

And if you can't be light hearted, then at least be real. Perhaps that's even more important.

Don't be afraid to be personal! Most people are eager to talk about themselves. And my experience is that people find answering personal questions a refreshing relief. I think that people who are successful in having lots of relationships and long-term relationships — well, it has something to do with being personal. Oh yes — you should know that when you're asking a personal question, you also have to be willing to *answer* personal questions.

Dolly Parton doesn't seem ever to lack for things to say. And I've noticed, whenever I've seen her interviewed on TV, that she's very willing to answer any and all personal questions. This seems to make her very attractive and popular. So ask questions of the person next to you. If you're interested in knowing them, ask about them.

I'm going to give you some examples of openers. Some of them might seem very outrageous, and you may wonder if they aren't too personal or too fast, but *how much time do you have to waste?* In a grocery store you don't have much time to connect — you've *got* to be speedy. I know a man who went up to a woman at a grocery store and said: "I'm a single man, I've noticed you here several times, and I wonder if we might have coffee together after we do our shopping." Well, they did. Simple as that.

When I talk to the people in my class, they all say they would feel wonderful if someone approached *them* — even if they didn't want to go out with that person, they would still feel good and wouldn't be offended. In fact...

MOST PEOPLE WISH MORE PEOPLE WOULD APPROACH THEM **MORE OFTEN**

So here are some ideas for openers. Use mine for ideas and then put on your thinking caps and create some more.

The excuse, "I couldn't think of a thing to say," may solace you but it doesn't *give* you anything, doesn't enhance your life, doesn't work.

Conversation Starters

Now don't be shocked if some of them seem too personal. That's the idea! You *want* to get the conversation going in a personal direction. Asking personal questions not only lets people know you're interested in being personal, it's also a way of **_screening people,_** testing them and checking them out. After all, you don't want to wait months to discover that someone has tastes and values that are totally different from your own — do you? That would be a very uneconomical use of time. Instead, you want to know as much about the other person as you can in the *shortest* possible time. So remember that what you're doing is *asking questions that screen out the people you're not interested in.* OK? So go ahead and

Ask questions that screen out *the people you're not interested in!*

Let's say you're sitting next to someone at a counter in a restaurant or you're standing in line for tickets to a concert. Well, after you've said "Pass the salt" or commented on the long line, what do you say next? *How do you keep the conversation going while letting the person know you're not just being polite and filling up space?*

Here's how:

- *"Do you own a computer?"*

The idea is that you want to ask them about something that you are interested in. So *you* need to keep the conversation going even if they don't keep up the conversation. For example, if in answer to the above question they simply say "No," you might ask, "Are you *interested* in computers?" Or you might just say, "Well then, what are you interested in?" (If they're not interested in *anything*, the best thing is to forget about them — they certainly won't be interested in *you!*)

Here are some questions that will tell you to what extent it's OK to be personal :

- *"Do you think it's OK for people to be personal when they first meet each other?"*
- *"Have you ever placed an ad in the personals?"* And if they haven't, you say: *"Have you ever thought about it?"*
- *"I'm conducting a survey. Do you think people should always tell the truth? Do you?"*

A good approach is to use the vast range of **"Have you ever...?"** questions:

- *"Have you ever wanted to be a writer?"*
- *"Have you ever wanted to be an entrepreneur?"*
- *"Have you ever wanted to be famous?"*
- *"Have you ever wanted to live in a foreign country? Why? Why haven't you?"*

- *"Have you ever wanted to be a benefactor of humanity? How would you go about it?"*
- *"Have you ever wanted to have it all? What would you do if you did?"*

Obviously there are lots more — you can let your imagination go to town on this one.

- *"Do you believe in talking to strangers?"*
- *"How many credit cards do you own?"*
- *"Are you single?"* (If they answer *"Yes,"* say *"So am I! How do you like being single?"* If they answer *"No,"* say *"Why don't you tell me about some of your single friends?"*)

If asking the above question seems too direct, you might say: *"I notice you're not wearing a wedding ring."* Which is not a question but a simple and gentle statement. Won't it be interesting to see how they handle that one?

If you meet someone at a restaurant or luncheonette:

- *"Do you eat here often?"*
- *"Which is your favorite restaurant?"*
- *"May I give you my business card?"* (Be sure to get one of theirs.)

- *"Do you think it's OK for people to talk about religion?"*
- *"How long do you think people who are attracted to one another ought to wait to have sex?"*
- *"When was the last time you were in love?"*
- *"I'm starting a discussion group, are you interested in discussions? Would you like to join?"*
- *"Would you like to go on a picnic?"* (If they say *"But it's raining,"* tell them: *"The picnic is going to be in the living room!"*)
- *"Do you have enough men/women in your life?"*
- *"Are you enjoying yourself today?"*
- *"How's your life going?"* or *"What's your life been like?"*

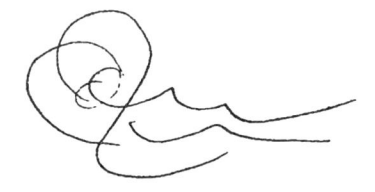

Avoid presumptous questions. Say: "I'd like to talk with you more. Can we do that another time?" Don't say: "I'd like to talk with you more, *when* can we do that?" That's making an unwarranted assumption. There are people who succeed with such questions, but only because they intimidate people, and when you intimidate people, you'll reap what you sow — sooner or later.

Avoid "what do you think of?" questions, at least at first. They get you into your head and lead to arguments. Also, they are not really personal. I am always more interested in what someone *likes* than in what they think. That's a much better guide to who you're going to feel good with.

Avoid questions that are quantitative and can be answered in numbers — "how many," "how often," etc. Remember that you are not after numbers — you are after *warmth!* Ask about the numbers *after* you get the warmth. If you're the kind of person who puts the numbers first, chances are you'll soon be coming in for counseling.

Here are questions for class room situations:

- *"Why did you decide to take this class?"*
- *"Was there any other class you were thinking of taking?"*

Another category is the "or" range of questions:

- *"Would you rather be rich or famous?"*
- *"Are your closets at home neat or messy?"*
- *"Do you prefer wine or beer?"*

And don't forget the **"How do you feel about...?"** range:

- *"How do you feel about shy, lonesome men?"*
- *"How do you feel about forward women?"*
- *"How do you feel about small talk?"*

Here are still others:

- "Have you ever been in Amway?"
- Have you ever been in a cult?"
- "Have you ever studied Eastern Religions?"
- "Do you like dancing? Would you teach me to dance, or can I teach you?"
- "Do you like children?"
- "Do you ever buy lottery tickets? What would you do if you won?"
- "Do you like window shopping?"
- "Do you like potluck dinners?"
- "Do you like bubble baths?"
- "Are you good with your hands?"
- "Where do you go to meet men/women?"

If you're stuck for what to say, remember that a great opening line is simply, "*Hello, my name is* _____ ." Look the person right in the eye and smile! If you want to make a lasting impression, hold out your hand, but instead of a business handshake, give a soft squeeze — preferably with both hands!

Now just imagine that you're in a room or elevator. You're with somebody you want to say something to and you don't want them to get away without making contact — and all of a sudden your mind goes totally blank. You simply can't think of a thing to say! *Well, memorize this and say it:*

> "I want to say something
> to you
> but my mind just went blank."

They'll probably understand and help you out.

AN IMPORTANT RULE TO REMEMBER. When you ask to see someone again, ***don't be vague!*** Instead of saying, "Let's get together sometime," be more specific. Say: "How about brunch on Saturday or tennis on Sunday?" Be specific and offer them some alternatives! Of course, that's riskier because you might get rejected, but it's a risk that often pays off. Oh, and when you leave a message on someone's answering machine, let them know *when* they can call you back. Say: "I'll be in Thursday evening from eight to ten."

THE REJECTION EXERCISE

Or

Learning Not To Feel Bad
When Someone Turns You Down

In the course I teach, **How to Find a Lover**, I find that one of the most frequent concerns is about being *rejected.* When I suggest places to go and things to try and new things to say, people worry that they may get rejected. And people quite naturally want to *avoid* rejection. But if you do that, there won't be many new lovers in your life. So instead, *isn't it better to get more comfortable with rejection?* It really is not such a big deal anyway.

I know it's very hard to get rejected — it feels bad. People are very afraid of getting rejected. *But the more you get rejected, the closer you are to success.*

Ask any successful salesman and they will tell you that they and their products are rejected more often than they are accepted — and yet they're still successful. In spite of having more rejections than acceptances, they are successful.

Many, many famous books were rejected *many* times before they ever got published. Some by over twenty publishers! Ayn Rand's *The Fountainhead*, a highly successful novel, was rejected by a dozen publishers. *Catch-22* was rejected, *From Here To Eternity* was rejected and — listen to this — even the immensely successful *How To Win Friends And Influence People* was rejected.

Now, can you imagine someone like Dale Carnegie giving up just because he received a rejection slip in the mail?

Think of it this way: a book can be rejected many, many times — by many, many publishers. *But if just one publisher accepts that book, why then it's published and could just become a best seller.* And when that happens, won't those publishers who rejected the book be sorry?

You see, **success is not a popularity contest!** Yes, a majority elects the president, but it takes only *one* publisher's approval to launch a book — *and only one person's appreciation to launch a happily married spouse.*

I know many happy and deeply loved wives who weren't popular with other men at all, *ever*. The point is, you see, that the *majority* simply doesn't have any say in affairs of the heart.

Yes, my friends,

IN AFFAIRS OF THE HEART...
THE MAJORITY DOESN'T COUNT

So if you want to have new people in your life, remember that the more rejections you get, the closer you are to winning the jackpot!

And I think if you keep this in mind, it will make rejections a little easier to take.

When you are rejected, there will probably be a sting. That is natural. You'll probably feel like crying, and you'll feel a little blue, and you could even be mad as hell.

This is all right. This is good. Feeling these things will help you handle future rejection without being devastated. **It's OK to cry when you're rejected and feel depressed** — and it's OK to be angry — but it's *not* OK to beat yourself up! It's *not* OK to feel you're a rotten, lousy person. Or that there isn't any hope for you.

When you're rejected, avoid the tendency to take out the whip and beat yourself. *Please* don't call yourself names. Know that rejection is *part* of success. In fact, *you can't arrive at success without overcoming your fear of rejection.* Otherwise you'd *continue* to fear rejection, and that fear would tarnish your happiness.

Here are some...

Mental Steps For Dealing With Rejection:

1. The more rejections, the closer you are to success.
2. Understand that you *will* be rejected — it's part of the process.
3. There is always a little sting to rejection, but if it's more than a sting, you're beating yourself up, and that's counter-productive.
4. When you feel the sting, it is OK to cry, feel blue, or get mad.
5. If you do that, eventually, you'll be able to laugh about it even while you're crying — or cursing.
6. Get your feelings out so you can be prepared for your next rejection — and your next success!
7. Raving and ranting are definitely far better ways of coping than overeating or other forms of "stuffing it."

Remember, *rejection equals success.* It really does.

Look at it this way: 1 + 1 equals 2, doesn't it? Well, and so does 4 minus 2! And 6 divided by 3. The point I'm making is there are many ways, *many* roads, to your outcome — and *rejection*, believe it or not, might actually be one of them. Really!

Believe me, friends, I have been rejected, dejected, squashed, squelched, deceived, ignored, betrayed and stomped on — and that is why I am a success today! So *rejoice* in your rejections.

HOMEWORK

The Rejection Exercise

How do you get more comfortable with rejection? Easy — *by getting rejected!* Read books by or on millionaires and they will all tell you about their rejections. So if you want to succeed, learn to handle rejection by doing the rejection exercise. Here it is:

At least three times a day,

try to get rejected.

That's right, you didn't misread the small print!

Try to get rejected

***three* times each day**

by trying a new approach

and talking to a Brand New Person...

Will you try that? *Yes?* Oh, but before you start, here's a word of warning.

If you try this exercise daily, you may sometimes find yourself accepted — and that can be really scary. *Yes, sometimes it is actually more scary to get accepted than to be rejected* — so don't say I didn't warn you.

Also, one of the worst things is that many of us have trained ourselves not to feel emotional pain. The pain is still there in our body, but we don't feel it as an emotion — instead we get back pains, headaches, or an ulcer. This "painless pain" takes the form of contractions in our stomach, our blood vessels, and our breathing and can in time lead to all sorts of illnesses, unfortunately. So what I say to you is that

> **FEELING REJECTED IS BETTER THAN NOT FEELING anything**

Yes, if you never take a chance, and if you don't learn to rant and rave, you'll end up feeling *nothing!* You'll feel bored and alone! So please take a chance. Try something new, and when you do get rejected, just try something new again and *again* and **AGAIN**. It really is worth it.

Love Making & Sex

I was watching a movie on TV the other day. It was called *Carnal Knowledge* and starred Jack Nicholson and it was about sexual attitudes in the Fifties. It was about two college students. One of them kept asking the other for advice on 'how to handle women.' He would ask, "and what should I do if she does this, and what should I do if she does that," you know, that kind of thing. And the character who was played by Jack Nicholson said, "By the third date you should have your hand on her _____ ." The word was blooped out, which was strange because the movie actually showed him putting his hand on her _____ . *That* wasn't blooped out!

Now here was a young man who thought the only way to relate to a girl was sexually! He had learned that from his friends and, I guess, from certain kinds of magazines. Do you know that some men, when they have dates, actually ask each other questions like, *"Did you get laid yet?"* And I've known women who do that too, although the words they use are usually a little more delicate.

A lot of people feel this has gone too far and they say we have to do something about pornography. And their way of dealing with it is censorship, and I don't think this works. *I don't think suppression and a 'don't' attitude ever work.*

I think the way to deal with pornography and pornographic attitudes is to make people understand the immense joy of love-making — ***and by love-making I don't necessarily mean sex.***

I have made love with people in stores, in shopping malls, on trains, at business conferences — people whose names I didn't know, people I never saw again. Sometimes we actually physically touched and more times we didn't. Sometimes we spoke and sometimes we didn't. But whether we touched or made love from afar, let me tell you, neither of us was in any doubt that we were in fact making love.

I have called up people I've seen on TV and gotten to know them, simply because they were making love right there in front of the TV cameras! I once watched a man talking about a toothpaste he had developed. Well, I called that man up and we became friends, simply because he was making love and I could feel it!

Many of you have children. And I'm sure you know the thrill that comes when you're really talking with your child, and you start to chortle about something, and soon tears are running down your eyes, you're both laughing so hard. Well, what do you think that is? *It's making love!*

See, we have all had these experiences. I don't think there is anybody who hasn't had these experiences. The trouble is we always think the other person is having something better, so we tend to feel we're missing out.

I assure you I am not against sex. But not everything has to be sexual. If what you really want is sex, then I say go into it, go for it, get all you want and *enjoy it* as long as it's still in your system.

Now here's a little story I want to share with you:

THE SHRIMP GIRL

I once knew a girl who had a craving for shrimp, and she decided that rather than eat shrimp now and then and here and there, she was going to eat shrimp all the time as much as she wanted. And she did. **She ate shrimp in the morning and she ate shrimp for lunch and she had it for dinner.** She mixed it with other things of course — she had shrimp in salads and she had shrimp fried in a batter and so on — but the point is, she totally went into it. She gave herself permission to eat shrimp any time she felt like it. And just that fact alone — the fact that she had given herself permission to do something that normally is just never done — that fact alone made her feel great!

Well, what do you think happened? Do you think she still eats shrimp all the time? *Do you think she has become a shrimpomaniac?* No, of course not. One day she got tired of her shrimp binge. She wasn't drawn to it anymore. Shrimp no longer had any special appeal to her — she had shrimped herself out! Oh, she still eats it occasionally but it is no longer an irresistible craving. Now, shrimp is simply a food that is available. It isn't on her mind anymore.

Some people will say, "Well I wouldn't want shrimp to become as ordinary as peanut butter. I *want* shrimp to always be a little special." I can understand that point of view — it's nice to have something special. I've had lovers who I only see once in a great while because I want them to remain special. That is completely understandable.

But let me tell you, even though I occasionally do this, I know that this is an expression of my lack of trust of what life has to offer. Because life has much more to offer than just shrimp or sex. There are many, *many* wonderful experiences we don't even have words for, and they're all available.

Some people will say, "Well, I like lobster and I can't afford lobster every day — lobster costs more than shrimp. What can I do about *that?*" And my answer is "Honey, there you go trying to be *logical* again! Why don't you just enjoy the lobster when you get it? And if you *never* get it, why not enjoy just thinking about it?"

See, I've discovered that you can enjoy life. Did you hear that? **I've discovered that you CAN actually enjoy life** — yes, people like you and me! You can enjoy even your tears and your misery. If you don't *have* something, you can enjoy thinking about it. You can enjoy thinking about lobster, and you *don't* have to bum yourself out because at the moment you don't have any.

Now there's one more thing I want to talk with you about here and that's

EXCUSES

I don't mean the excuses you make to someone else, I mean the excuses you make to yourself. I've noticed we have two kinds of excuses that we give ourselves: excuses for doing something and excuses for *not* doing something. And in my experience, the excuses we give ourselves for *not* doing something are the ones that eat us up the most. They just nag at us something terrible, don't they?

And do you know what we really have a hard time forgiving ourselves for? No, it's not *sinning*; we are usually quite able to forgive ourselves for that! But what we can't seem to forgive in our behavior is missing the moment, missing out on spontaneity. We can't seem to forgive ourselves for not doing the unexpected. Or, we can't forgive ourselves for *only* doing what's expected.

For example, have you ever overheard someone talking in a restaurant, and what they're saying touches you in some way? And you want to say hello to them, to this perfect stranger, to say, "Hey, I heard what you said and I think you're *wonderful,* and I want you to know I'm *with* you" — have you ever felt like that? And you know, you're afraid to, you're afraid that the other person may say, "So you were eavesdropping" or *"Who is this creep?!"* and get mad or put you down. Well, you can think about all the reasons you have for not doing that, not talking to them, or you can do that unexpected thing, make that unexpected move, and take your chances.

When you do the unexpected, life suddenly opens up for you.

In a way, that is the essence of what good love-making is all about — *giving yourself permission to do the unexpected.* When you give yourself that permission, you're not only making love to the other person, you're in a way making love to yourself.

Well, this is not just an *essay* — I'm not just telling you these things so you can say, "Well that sounds nice," yawn, and turn on the TV! I want you to start *doing* something about all this! So here are a few small steps that I want you to practice every day:

Flirt with someone,
catch the eye of a stranger,
tickle a baby's chin,
blow a kiss to a senior citizen,
give hugs and pats,
give winks,
LAUGH,
smile,
and walk with a skip...
**Look around and
do the unexpected —**
you'll find
there are lots of lovers
EVERYWHERE!

If you do this, you will find yourself attracting more and more people. And one of them might end up being super-special to you — that's your bonus!

But let me insert here a brief word of caution. Whether we like it or not, sexually transmitted diseases are part of our lives today. AIDS is a fact of life, and informed sources agree that it is going to get worse. But many of you reading this, like the people who come to my classes, have questions about just how do you approach this subject? *How* do you talk about it with someone with whom you want to have sex? Well, the only way to do this is to talk about it openly and directly. Or rather, *gently*, openly, and directly!

Begin by saying, "I want to talk to you about something important." Tell them that you've heard that sexually transmitted diseases are a big risk factor these days and ask, "Would you be willing to talk about this? Would you be willing to talk about your previous sexual partners?" You will also want to discuss with your new lover what precautions will best ensure safe sex.

Certainly no reasonable person will be offended at you for wanting to take steps that will protect both of you. Only an unreasonable person would mind your asking such questions. And unless you are self-destructive or a masochist, you will want to be with a person who is at least *reasonably* reasonable!

THOUGHTS TO CONSIDER

These are some important thoughts for you to consider:

• More than 50 million Americans are single. One out of every three adults between the ages of 20 - 55 are single. Life-long marriages seem to be becoming rarer every day.

• I have met unhappy married people and unhappy singles. I have met happy marrieds and happy singles. Regardless of your marital status, I would choose a little happiness.

• It is natural to want a relationship; it is also natural to be alone, to be single. We spend many years alone. So put some energy into being okay when you're with yourself. Be your *own* best lover, friend, and companion.

• If you don't love *yourself*, how do you think you're ever going to be able to love *others*?

• It is far better to yearn for a lover and to feel sad you don't have one than to pretend to yourself that you're okay without one. Only facing the truth will help you.

• Don't overlook the importance of friendship in your life. Don't just settle for casual acquaintances or pseudo-friends, but look for people who appreciate you, are supportive, and bring out **the best in you**.

Whether Looking For A Lover,
Friend Or Companion
ALWAYS REMEMBER, MY DEAR
FRIEND
**ALWAYS HOOK UP WITH PEOPLE
WHO
<u>BRING OUT THE BEST IN YOU</u>**
MAKE **YOUR** FRIENDS
THE PEOPLE WHO
BRING OUT THE BEST IN YOU

A PARTING WORD...

Before we part, there's one thing more I want to tell you about and that's...

"Looking For Lover Burn-Out"

I've told you just about everything I know about finding lovers and keeping them. And I truly believe — and know — it's possible to have fulfilling, loving relationships in your life. But frequently, in people's quest to have this happen, *they try so hard that they simply get burned out!* They get burned out when they don't succeed. And this can be very, very discouraging! So if this has happened to you and you feel discouraged, you may be suffering from burn-out syndrome or, more specifically, from

'Looking for Lover' Burn-Out Syndrome

As I told you when we began, this is not so much a 'how to' book as it really is a book of encouragement. There are plenty of books that tell you exactly what to do and what to say and what approaches to take. And all this can lead to what I call 'looking for lover burn-out.'

I think most people who have had periods of being alone have felt this. 'Looking for lover burn-out' happens when you've been looking and looking and going to all the right places (for months or even years) looking for a lover. And after all that effort, all that doing, nothing truly satisfying has happened. You bravely go to dance after dance, you go to hear this lecture and that lecture, and though you may have had zillions of dates, you're practically right where you started. You've talked about yourself to umpteen candidates and heard their life stories, you've memorized countless names and written down oh-so-many phone numbers, and still your soul has not been nourished.

Do I have to tell you how discouraging this can be? You yourself know far too well. You know how this sort of thing can make you wonder "What's wrong with me?" You know how much all this zaps your energy and erodes your spirit. So if you sense that you are getting discouraged, weary, tired of looking and sick of trying to figure it all out, then, my friend, you are experiencing **Burn-Out.**

And the best cure for this is simply to stop. *Stop* looking for lovers, *stop* thinking about what you could do or where to go to make 'it' happen. **Stop for a while, and don't worry.** You need a break. You need to heal yourself a little. Oh, and one more thing! Wonderful and unexpected things can happen — when you aren't even looking. When you've stopped your overly active seeking for your lover, your lover may just surprise you — and find *you!*

THAT'S RIGHT!
Dear friend,
when **YOU** stop
looking
trying
efforting
searching...
your lover
may
find
YOU!

Well, that's it. I think I have shared with you just about all I know about finding lovers, friends, and companions. I know it works. I like having men and women friends in my life, and I have done a lot of what I've shared, and it has brought me lots of experiences with people — some became friends, others were lovers, and some just passed through my life for a moment.

Oh, there is one last suggestion which has worked wonders for me. I invite people to dinner at my house. It is my way of saying to the other person: "I like you, lets get to know each other." This is my way of sharing part of me with someone I would like to know better.

**SO GOOD-BYE
AND GOOD LUCK
DON'T WORRY!
AND DON'T DELAY
YOU CAN FIND
A
LOVER
A
FRIEND
A
COMPANION**

P.S. HERE'S ANOTHER IMPORTANT IDEA

REALLY WORTH THINKING ABOUT!

We're all on a road travelling to somewhere, and we all have some sense of what we're moving towards. We have an idea of where we'd like to go, but sometimes we get so afraid that we think we'll never make it. I know people who hope they'll find a beautiful lover, but they're *afraid* they won't. Their fears take hold of them and smother their hopes.

Our hope for happiness gets dampened by our fears. Our optimism is crushed by our pessimism. If our fears are stronger than our optimistic expectations, we feel panicky because we're convinced we're going to be moving down instead of up. We foresee failure, yet we go on speaking the language of hope. I know people who throw their shoulders back and *talk* about being winners, but inside they think of themselves as losers. And I want to tell you that **our own impression of what we're moving toward can totally make the difference between happiness and unhappiness.** This is so important that I'll say it again:

Our Own Impression
Of What We're Moving
TOWARD
Can Totally Make
The Difference
Between HAPPINESS And
UNHAPPINESS

I have a friend who all her life has felt she is a "bad" and unattractive person. She would like to find a lover, and now and then she tries. But she confided to me one day, sobbing, that she feels there is no hope for her, that regardless of whatever efforts she makes, she will simply become more and more lonely as time goes by. She says she knows better, but she thinks of this as a kind of punishment for not being a really "good" person — for sometimes being spiteful and angry and so on. She is unhappy because of what *she* feels she is moving towards. Occasionally she even feels she will end her days destitute, abandoned, uncared for — maybe even a bag lady. And this thought haunts and torments her.

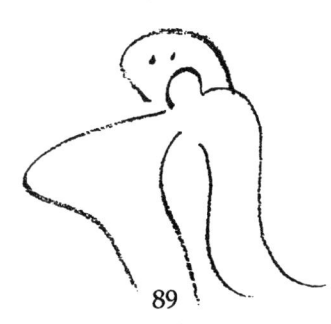

*What do **you** feel you are moving towards?* Even if you feel, like my friend, that there is no hope for you, I want to tell you that *the idea that there is no hope for you **is only a belief!*** It's only baggage that you're carrying around with you. So here's what I want you to do: I want you to sit down and put everything else out of your mind and **make contact with the essential goodness in you**, with that part of you that deep, deep, deep down *knows* you are a good and worthwhile person and truly deserving. And when you've done that, complete this statement — *and do it again and again until you really feel good about it:*

I AM MOVING TOWARDS...

_____

_____

_____

_____

_____

Make these statements both positive, realistic, and as clear and detailed and life-affirming as possible — for example,

"I am moving towards happiness."
"I am moving towards greater fulfillment."
"I am moving toward a relationship where I will feel truly appreciated."
"I am moving toward being loved for who I really am."
"I am moving toward more love than I have ever known before."
"I am moving toward a relationship of greater openness and trust in which there won't be any of the game playing that I've had in my previous relationships."
"I am moving toward a time of greater self-confidence."
"I am moving toward a growing sense of serenity of what life has to offer me."

There's still one final thought I want to leave you with — one that it took me a long time to discover, and that is that...

Lovers Are Luxuries!

Yes, lovers are *luxuries*. They are not necessities of life. Lovers are like chocolate or ice-cream. They add a lot of fun to life — a special flavor, but you *can* live without them. If you eat a steady diet of luxuries without the necessities, you'll soon get restless. You'll soon be craving something else.

It is like this: if you ate nothing but chocolate or ice-cream everyday, all day, you might enjoy it for a while, but it wouldn't take long and soon you would be craving bread and butter or maybe fruit or even *vegetables*. Well, lovers are like that. If you have a steady diet of them, without any of the necessities of life, you'll soon feel like you're missing something. Then you'll get restless and when you do, maybe you'll even start looking for the necessities of life.

Don't look to your lover to bring you the necessities! Make sure you can get those for yourself, then you'll be ready for some luxury. Provide your own necessities, and then have as much of the luxuries as you want.

You see, it's like this. There are lessons in life we all need to learn, and sometimes we need to be alone to learn those lessons, and sometimes we need to be a couple. And I have no idea which phase *you* are in, and you probably don't either. So it's important that you trust the process. *What process?* The process called life!

If you are alone,
then **trust** that this is where you need to be,
and when you need to be
with someone special,
a Magical Moment
will happen,
and you will *know* that it is time
to learn by being with another,
and you will *surely* find someone,
because that is how it was meant to be.

That is usually the way it happens. Like magic! All the good things of life come to us easily — provided that *we* don't get in the way! Just trust what I am saying here, and you'll do *far* better than if you struggled and strained and pushed. All the things in this book will help you in your life process, that I am sure of. Otherwise, I wouldn't write them.

So good-bye, dear friend. I've shared with you all I have learned about bringing lovers into your life. Remember that despite all trials and tribulations, love is what makes life worth living. **Always value your friendships, and never forget to have time for friends.** I know that you can have what you want in your life.

Be well, *celebrate* your life, and please let me know what happens!

Love,

Judy

Judy Ford is a lively, enthusiastic parent whose motto is "never a dull moment." She is also a human relations consultant, a counselor in private practice, and a popular professional speaker. Judy's zest for living and her sparkle when she enters a room are immediately contagious — even when she is down. She loves to encounter people, to challenge them in a good-natured way, and to be challenged in turn. Her weekly radio show *"Life, Love and Relationships"* is attracting increasing attention.

Judy has given talks to medical professionals, civic groups, and business organizations. The themes she likes to speak on include **Parenting**, a delightful lecture in which Judy encourages parents to recognize their children's wisdom, **Courageous Living**, in which Judy shares her experiences of loss and tells of her successful struggle to create a life full of joy, creativity, and celebration, **Discovering Your Uniqueness**, a high energy romp in which Judy urges that your uniqueness is both fun and marketable, and **Living With A Teenager**, the title of her next book. Together with Dr. Ross, she frequently writes articles on relationships for a leading women's magazine. She is president of Judy Ford & Company, a company devoted to developing products and offering talks, workshops, and seminars that deal with love, relationships, healing, and playful wisdom.

William Ashoka Ross is a gentle man with a sparkle in his eye. A psychotherapist for almost twenty years, he now helps people integrate meditation with love energy, truth-telling, and self-assertion. He is the author of **"Lovers' Quarrels: The Other Side Of Romance," "Sex: There's More To It Than You've Been Told,"** and **"Words From The Masters: A Guide To The God Within."**

Lovers' Quarrels: The Other Side Of Romance is a collection of ordinary and extraordinary scenes and squabbles that put the freeze on intimacy and chill affections. Here are the situations your friends and neighbors will never tell you about! These fights, also known as "impasses," are due to breakdowns in communication caused by highly charged sore spots. Never have so many of these blow-by-blow dramas been collected before. Reading these scenarios — 127 little stories like *Late For Dinner, Honesty Punished, Sexual Bliss, Other Woman, Switcheroo* and *Mamma Knows Best* — we learn to view ourselves with a humor and compassion that will enhance our appreciation of our own relationships. *Charming, insightful, and beautifully illustrated!*

Sex: There's More To It Than You've Been Told is a wonderful book of insights about love and sex! "It has the effect of a gentle massage that eases away your tensions so that you can see sex as it could be in your life: relaxed, vital, renewing, a deep expression of a loving self." "A collection of clear, pithy and often witty observations." Talk show host: "Don't be dismayed at the seemingly small size of this little jewel; it's packed with thoughts, attitudes and information that can make a real difference." **The Chicago Tribune** calls it "a celebration of the healthful benefits of loving sexual relations." A nurse: "Makes you feel like celebrating and starting life all over again!" Therapist: *"A wonderful communication tool for couples!"*

Lovers' Quarrels: The Other Side... $4.95 plus $1 p.&h.
Sex: There's More To It... $4.95 plus $1 p.&h.

Send check or money order to:
Playful Wisdom Press
PO Box 834, Kirkland, WA 98083
For information call 206/ 823-4421